Venus

Lori Dittmer

CREATIVE EDUCATION
CREATIVE PAPERBACKS

seedlings

Published by Creative Education and Creative Paperbacks
P.O. Box 227, Mankato, Minnesota 56002
Creative Education and Creative Paperbacks
are imprints of The Creative Company
www.thecreativecompany.us

Design by Ellen Huber; production by Joe Kahnke
Art direction by Rita Marshall
Printed in the United States of America

Photographs by Alamy (Stephen Emerson, National Geographic
Creative), Black Cat Studios (Ron Miller), Creative Commons
Wikimedia (Sandro Botticelli/Uffizi Gallery), NASA (NASA/JPL),
Science Source (David Hardy, Detlev van Ravenswaay, Take 27 Ltd),
Shutterstock (janez volmajer), SuperStock (Science Photo Library)

Library of Congress Cataloging-in-Publication Data
Names: Dittmer, Lori, author.
Title: Venus / Lori Dittmer.
Series: Seedlings.
Includes bibliographical references and index.
Summary: A kindergarten-level introduction to the planet
Venus, covering its orbital process, its moons, and such
defining features as its volcanoes, heat, and name.
Identifiers: ISBN 978-1-60818-920-5 (hardcover) / ISBN 978-1-
62832-536-2 (pbk) / ISBN 978-1-56660-972-2 (eBook)
This title has been submitted for CIP
processing under LCCN 2017938984.

CCSS: RI.K.1, 2, 3, 4, 5, 6, 7;
RI.1.1, 2, 3, 4, 5, 6, 7; RF.K.1, 3; RF.1.1

First Edition HC 9 8 7 6 5 4 3 2 1
First Edition PBK 9 8 7 6 5 4 3 2 1

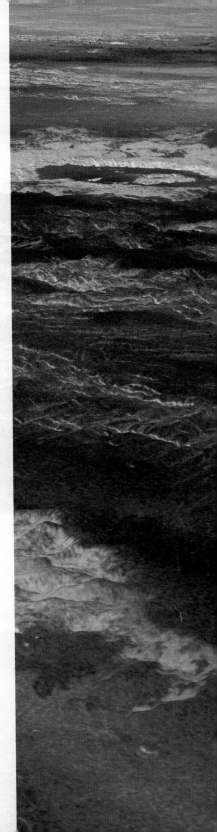

TABLE OF CONTENTS

Hello, Venus!

Venus is the second planet from the sun. It is gray and rocky. But the air around it makes it look orange.

A thick blanket of gases and clouds covers Venus.

The blanket traps heat.
This makes Venus the
hottest planet!

Venus is close
to Earth.
Sometimes,
you can see
it at night.
It looks like
a bright star.

Venus is about the same size as Earth. It has many volcanoes.

It takes Venus 225 days to orbit the sun.

Astronomers study planets. They found Venus thousands of years ago. They named it for an old story about the goddess of love.

Clouds swirl.
Lightning
flashes. The
sky is hazy.

Goodbye, Venus!

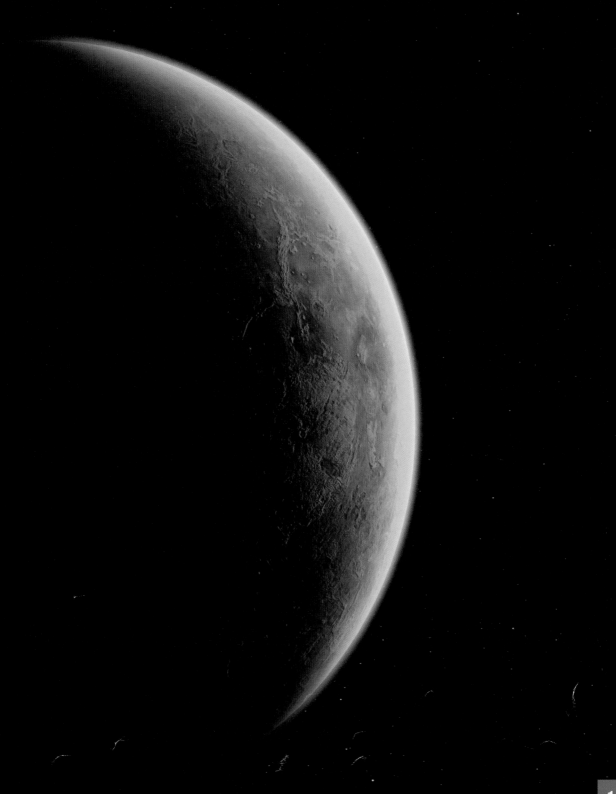

Picture Venus

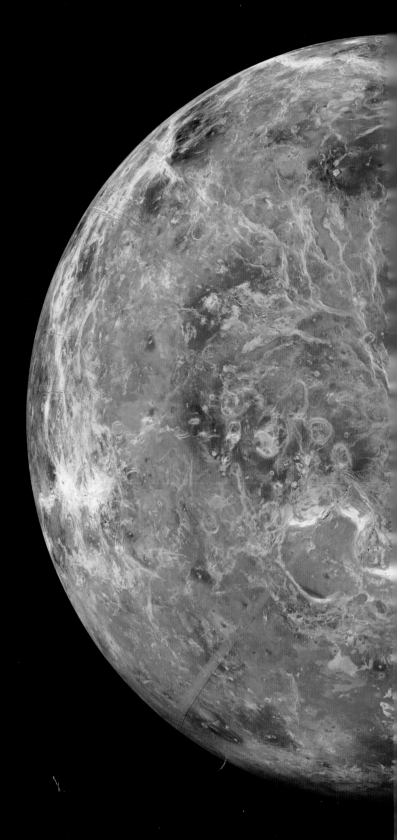

surface

rocks

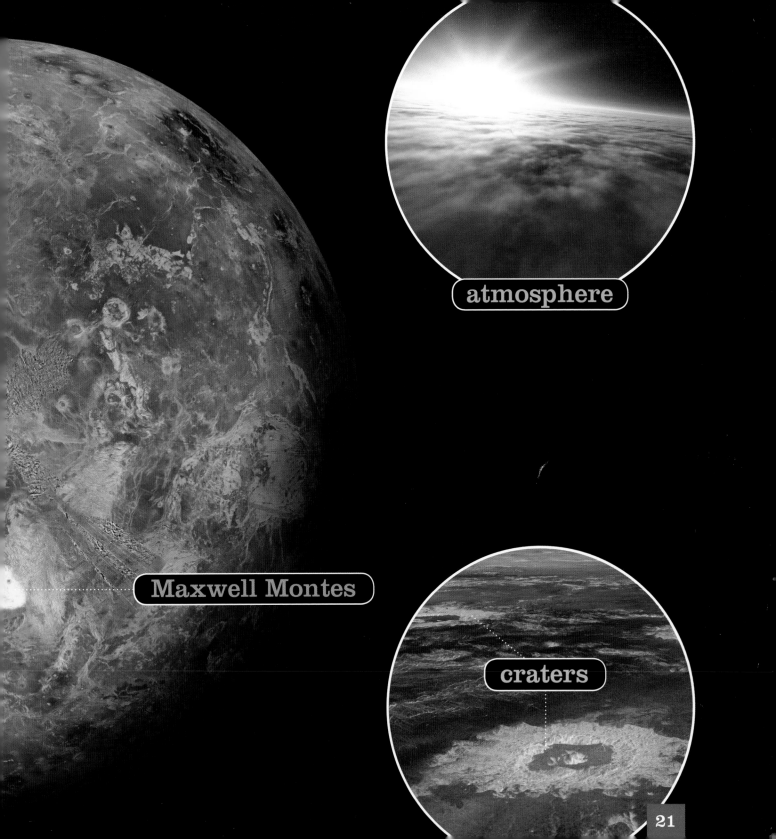

atmosphere

Maxwell Montes

craters

goddess: a being thought to have special powers and control over the world

orbit: the path a planet, moon, or other object takes around something else in outer space

planet: a rounded object that moves around a star

volcanoes: mountains with a hole on top that sometimes sends out rocks, ash, and lava

Read More

Adamson, Thomas K. *Do You Really Want to Visit Venus?* Mankato, Minn.: Amicus, 2014.

Loewen, Nancy. *Brightest in the Sky: The Planet Venus.* Minneapolis: Picture Window Books, 2008.

Websites

NASA Jet Propulsion Laboratory: Kids
http://www.jpl.nasa.gov/kids/
Build a spacecraft or play a planetary game.

National Geographic Kids: Mission to Venus
http://kids.nationalgeographic.com/explore/space/mission
-to-venus/#venus-planet.jpg
Learn how Venus moves through our solar system.

Index